R&D's Role in Product Liability

Frank C. Jose, Jr.

American Management Association, Inc.

This book has been distributed without charge to AMA members enrolled in the R&D Division.

International standard book number: 0–8144–2137–7
Library of Congress catalog card number: 75–109525

Contents

1 Product Liability Today 5

2 Prevention: Precomplaint Action 14

3 Discovery and Disposition: Complaint Investigation and Termination 26

4 Two Agrichemical Case Studies 50

Notes 62

About the Author 64

I

Product Liability Today

As NATIONAL, state, and local attention focuses more and more on the liabilities of manufacturers who are placing products into the stream of commerce, the role of research and development continues to grow in importance in the area of product liability complaints. It is true that this function assumes only a small percentage of research and development's overall workload and basic objectives, but it must not be underestimated, particularly in the light of manufacturers' commitments to produce defect-free products and to keep losses resulting from product liability complaints to a minimum. Indeed, research and development's contribution to these objectives is not generally given the recognition that is its due. The extent to which a company is successful in maintaining control of costs in this sphere of operations depends directly upon the time and effort that the company devotes to the problem of developing defenses against claims and lawsuits based on the production, sale, and use of its products.

It has been reported that American business and industry paid out a grand total of $17.3 billion for research and development in 1968. This is double the amount spent ten years ago. There are about 5,500 firms that operate research and development departments of their own, compared with the 4,100 of ten years ago. One of the many factors leading to this growth has been the increasing role it is being called upon to play in the handling of product liability complaints, a management responsibility that once lay entirely within the legal, insurance, or company claims department. Research and development's primary function remains the creation of new products, but the discovery of new processes, materials, and techniques makes its role increasingly significant in the handling of product liability losses.

Additional evidence of this increased activity is borne out by the recent announcement that manufacturers and contractors in 27 states would be paying more for liability insurance as of October 1, 1969, according to the insurance rating board's revised rate scales, which, with few exceptions, reflect substantial increases. The states with largest increases include California, where bodily injury rates are up 30 percent and property damage rates are up 20 percent; Louisiana, where bodily injury rates are up 65 percent and property damage up 25 percent; and Michigan, where bodily injury rates are up 30 percent and property damage 15 percent.[1*]

Company defense counsel, in an effort to evaluate the product liability claim or lawsuit, and determine the causal relationship between the company's product and the alleged injuries or damages, must of necessity rely heavily upon the opinions of the members of the research and de-

* All notes to the text are to be found at the end of the book.

velopment group. In the final analysis, it is upon the technical representatives of the research and development department that the company's legal counsel must rely to present the difficult scientific evidence to the court and jury. It is the task of these technical representatives to convert the language of the technologist to the language of the lay jury so that the evidence is readily understandable. This is no small accomplishment. The participation of research and development in the product liability field is as varied as the techniques used to accomplish its objectives; its functions run the gamut from conducting the technical aspects of the original investigation to providing witnesses at the trial, which is usually the final chapter in any product liability case history.

The extent of such participation is contingent upon the size and makeup of the company's research and development department. A typical research group in a large chemical company, for example, may run about 250 employees, more than 100 of whom are professionally trained biologists, chemists, and physiologists. The various scientific abilities of these specialists are called upon as the need arises to investigate the technical aspects of a complaint resulting from use of a company product. Having participated in the original development of the product, they are well equipped to seek out and ascertain the answers to the numerous complex questions that arise when a complaint is filed.

One statement about which there can be little dispute is that the volume of claims and lawsuits stemming from product liability is constantly growing. Undoubtedly, one of the greatest contributing causes is national advertising, which has made the public's demand for newer products insatiable. Along with this, of course, is the feeling on the part of the public that when a product has caused damage or injury, someone should pay for it. The public's awareness of its avenues of recovery against manufacturers has been aided in part by more liberal decisions by the courts; public policy now holds the manufacturer to a higher standard than one of due care. The question is not just a legal one of liability, but rather a social one of who is in the better position to distribute the risk.[2]

Government Participation

A factor that has contributed to the rise in interest in product liability is reflected in government participation. On December 20, 1967, a national commission on product safety was established, whose duty it would be to conduct a "comprehensive study and investigation of the scope and adequacy of measures now employed to protect consumers against unreasonable risk of injuries which may be caused by hazardous household products." The study was to consider the identity of categories of household products representing unreasonable danger; the protection afforded by self-regulation in industry; the protection afforded against hazardous products by common law; and the extent of federal, state, and local laws—including scope of coverage, effectiveness of sanctions, adequacy of investigatory powers, uniformity of application, and quality of enforcement. Here again we find pressure being put on research and development groups.

Still additional pressure being put on manufacturers is evidenced by President Nixon's October 30, 1969, request of Congress for a buyer's bill of rights. If passed, this bill would permit consumers to sue in federal court for damages resulting from fraudulent or deceptive trade practices. The suits, brought individually or by groups of consumers sharing the cost of the litigation, would be based on a proposed broad new federal law banning frauds and deceptions. The Federal Trade Commission's mandate would be expanded, and a new Justice Department division for consumer protection would be created under an assistant attorney general to enforce the law in the same way that a separate division enforces antitrust statutes. However, in a special message to Congress, President Nixon said that, in order to prevent harassment of legitimate businessmen by unlimited nuisance lawsuits, individual or group loss suits for damages could be filed only after the government itself had successfully sued to halt a violation of the law.

The President said that his proposed legislation, to be submitted later, was intended particularly to insure quick federal protection for low-income families, who are frequently victimized by unfair trade practices. For example, consumers now have no right to sue in federal court to recover the cost of a faulty refrigerator, and state laws against fraud or deception are often inadequate or nonexistent.

The President's plan to give legal muscle to the nation's store customers was the highlight of a message that also proposed the following measures:

1. The creation of a new White House Office of Consumer Affairs to coordinate all federal consumer-protection activities and relay citizen complaints to appropriate government agencies for action.
2. The amendment of current laws to give the FTC jurisdiction over activities *affecting* interstate commerce as well as those *in* interstate commerce. He

also proposed giving the FTC power to issue preliminary injunctions to halt unfair trade practices promptly.

3. The reexamination by the Food and Drug Administration of all substances now classified as "generally recognized as safe," in view of recent findings of adverse effects of the cyclamate artificial sweeteners.
4. The regular publication of a consumer bulletin that would explain technical information to the layman, as well as evaluation reports on products bought by the government, from light bulbs to automobile tires.
5. The immediate start of an investigation, by a commission established by Congress last year, of consumer credit that now totals $110 billion nationwide, and of the effectiveness of existing protection against unfair credit practices.

It is obvious that, even if only a small portion of these proposed programs become effective, there will be a considerable increase in activity in many phases of the products field. Manufacturers now faced with mounting litigation costs in the product liability field must also anticipate more appearances before federal courts and agencies. For example, it is believed that the proposed Justice Department unit would have a staff of about 50 lawyers and economists.

It should perhaps be noted that Ralph Nader, the consumer advocate, criticized the President's recommendations as deceptive and a "slick Madison Avenue package." He said that the consumer message was "filled with a program for future studies, future recommendations, and no present action." He specifically opposed placing a consumer unit in the Justice Department, because, he said, that department is too "politically oriented."

Strict Liability Doctrine

Manufacturers' responsibility in the product liability arena has moved in the past 20 years to fall within the scope of the strict liability doctrine. Simply put, this doctrine holds that a manufacturer is liable without fault if he sells a defective product. Liability for a product that causes physical harm is imposed upon the manufacturer, even though he may have used all possible care in producing the product. It is clear that widespread adoption of this doctrine increases the company's exposure to more claims and lawsuits, and subjects research and development to greater pressures to insure that the company's products are defect-free. Acceptance of this doctrine is justified on the grounds that public policy demands that loss associated with a product causing injuries and property damage should be borne by those who manufacture and market the product, and should be considered as an item in the cost of production. Among those who have been found subject to the strict liability doctrine are manufacturers of aircraft, automobiles, trucks, boats, forklifts, golfcarts, house trailers, tires, batteries, and insecticides.

However, it should be noted that the liability is not absolute. Instead, it eliminates the requirement of proof of fault as to the existence of a "defect," and requires that the "defect" be one that creates an unreasonable risk of harm to the user. Manufacturer's liability is dependent upon whether the product is fit (safe) or unfit (unsafe). Manufacturers must market a reasonably fit and merchantable product; otherwise they are "strictly" liable. The judgment in one case held that

> He [the manufacturer of a defective truck] can appropriately be held liable for physical injuries caused by defects requiring his goods to match a standard of safety defined in terms of conditions that create unreasonable risk of harm.[3]

The dissent in this case pointed out that this decision did not introduce a notion of "defective," which is different from that of "unmerchantable" in implied warranty law.

Under the strict liability in tort doctrine, as in the case of express or implied warranty of fitness or merchantability, proof of the manufacturer's negligence in the making or handling of the article is not required. If the article is defective—for example, not reasonably fit for the ordinary purposes for which such articles are sold and used; and if the defect arose from the design or manufacture, or while the article was in the control of the manufacturer; and if it proximately causes injury or damage to the ultimate purchaser or reasonably expected consumer—then liability exists.[4]

A decision given in Arkansas in 1949 involved the case of a chemical dust that had been used to spray certain crops from an airplane. The dust proved harmful to broad-leaved plants, and the plaintiff's cotton crop was damaged by drift of the dust application. The defendant's scientific experts testified that the company had had no prior experience of such a situation, although the defendant's research and development group admitted that it had made no test of the floating quality of the dust. The court decided for the plaintiff; while it did not base its decision on the defendant's failure to test, clearly it could have done so. Instead, it ruled against the defendant on the theory of strict liability for damage caused by a hazardous product. It commented:

> If one casts into the air a substance which he knows may do damage to others and in some circumstances will certainly do so, principles of elementary justice as well as the best public policy require that he know how far the substance will carry or be conveyed through the air and what damage it will do in the path of its journey, and if he releases such a substance with either ignorance or indifference to the damage that may be done, the rule of strict liability should be applied.
>
> We do not think [the defendant] excused itself from liability by the mere showing that it was unaware of the peculiar carrying quality of the dust it was selling. Ordinary care required that it should know, in view of the dangerous nature of the product it was selling, and it was charged with the knowledge which tests would have revealed. The case is, therefore, one in which the rule of strict liability should be applied.[5]

It is the general consensus that if the company in this case had conducted sufficient tests through its research and development group, the rule of strict liability would not have been applied. This would most likely have been true even if adequate tests had not revealed the hazards.

In another case, the inherent qualities of Sparine, a tranquilizing drug that would adversely affect only a small segment of the public, were found to render the drug "not unreasonably fit for human consumption."[6] A judgment involving cigarettes held that public policy had not decreed absolute liability for the harmful effects that no developed skill or foresight could avoid, and that the manufacturer was not the insurer against the unknowable risk.[7]

2

Prevention: Precomplaint Action

THE functions performed by research and development in the area of product liability claims fall into three principal phases: prevention, or precomplaint action; discovery, or complaint investigation; and disposition, or complaint termination. Many actions that are taken in the precomplaint stage will effectively avoid or minimize problems of product liability complaints.

Recent decisions of federal and state courts have emphasized the extent to which a company's liability can be determined by the research and development department's activity in the precomplaint period. Some of the major functions that have either a direct or an indirect bearing on the court's ultimate decision include the extent of test work prior to making the product available to the public, and such informational materials as labels, brochures, and pamphlets.

Part of the decision in the chemical case referred to in Chapter 1 stated that a manufacturer is bound by duty to exercise due care in the making of reasonable inspections and tests to discover any hazards, both patent and latent. However, this duty involves using reasonable care in making reasonable tests, and does not require the manufacturer to make tests that are not practical or economically feasible in relation to the risk.[8]

Manufacturers have been found liable in such cases as that in which a chair manufacturer failed to discover a defect in metal casting that would have been discernible through a careful visual examination,[9] or that in which the collapse of a bed upon normal use evidenced a failure to inspect or test.[10] In one case, it was shown that chemical and physical tests would have disclosed a defective semi-trailer kingpin.[11] In still another case, dealing with a chemical defoliant, the court declared that:

> Even if defendant [manufacturer of dust defoliant] had not failed to warn the public, as it was required to do by both federal and state law, defendant owed a common-law duty to make proper tests, give adequate warning, and in general protect the public from potential dangers arising out of the manufacture and sale of such hazardous materials.

In this case the defendant did not show that it had made sufficient tests to ascertain whether the product was safe to man; it was therefore held liable for marketing a product that was poisonous and thus ultrahazardous.[12]

Involved in the requirement that manufacturers test products is the fact that liability may be found even if there is no defect in the product. Courts have said that a manufacturer has a constant duty to make reasonable tests and inspections in order to give adequate warnings of dangers inherent even in defect-free products.[13] Thus a manufacturer is faced with the difficult task of being liable for unknown dangers in his product. One of the leading cases on this point was the Texas City disaster in which a fertilizer containing ammonium nitrate exploded.[14] No liability was found here, since the fertilizer had been produced and distributed at the instance of and according to plans under the control of the government. The court found that the need for further experimentation was a matter of discretion, and also that due care had been exercised.

As was pointed out in the dissent in this case, the scientific experts for the petitioner testified that, in their belief, at least a segment of informed scientific opinion at the time regarded ammonium nitrate as potentially dangerous, especially when combined with carbonaceous materials as it was in this case. One witness had been hired by the war production board to conduct tests on the explosion and fire hazards of the product. The board terminated these tests at an intermediate stage, against the recommendation of the laboratory and in the face of the suggestion that further research might point up suspected but unverified dangers. In addition, there had been a considerable history of unexplained fires and explosions involving ammonium nitrate over a period of years.

Despite the fact that manufacturers make tests and inspections, their duty is not discharged if these tests are inadequate—for example, if there is expert testimony that steel of improper grain size was used, and that the tests made by the defendant would not reveal the grain size of the metal.[15] Again, in a Michigan case involving a peach spray, tests had been made only in other states, although variances in climatic and soil conditions might cause different effects when the spray was used in Michigan.[16]

In another case, the plaintiff claimed that, in submitting a bid for construction of a sewer system, it had relied upon the soil testing report made by the defendant. This testing report had been intended by the defendant to provide information for prospective bidders such as the plaintiff, and had been made available to all bidders. Allegedly as a result of the defendant's negligence, the plaintiff's bid was $918,434 less than the actual cost. A summary judgment granted to the defendant was reversed on the grounds that the plaintiff's claim, if proved, would support the conclusion that the transaction had been intended to affect the plaintiff and was readily foreseeable, and that the plaintiff's loss was the direct result of the negligent soil analysis.[17]

The fact that a product may have been successfully used over a considerable period of time without previously resulting in injury does not necessarily provide a defense of an action:

> True, a manufacturer of an ordinarily safe article is not held to that degree of clairvoyance which hindsight alone can give. But, especially when injury is likely to be serious if trouble occurs, even slight foreseeability may warrant, and a long history of good fortune will not necessarily exclude, a conclusion by trier of the facts that prudence requires the manufacturer to take on so small an added burden.[18]

A very good question not clearly answered by the courts yet is: What is a manufacturer's liability if the research and development group has not been able to develop any test or inspection that is effective? Does a hazard warning on the label satisfy the responsibility of due care?

Research and development plays a critical role in the areas of labeling and of fulfilling the manufacturer's duty to warn. This duty presupposes that the manufacturer has knowledge of the possible harmful propensities of the company's products, and every manufacturer is held by the courts to possess expert knowledge through its research and development department. A manufacturer must give warning of any dangerous propensity that it knows to be inherent in its product, or in the product's use, particularly if the customer has no knowledge of the danger and would ordinarily not discover it. The research and development department is required to keep abreast of technological advances and scientific discoveries relating to its company's products.

Even though a product is perfectly made, the manufacturer has a duty to warn, and is under constant pressure to determine the extent to which it should warn. Some cases hold that the manufacturer has an additional duty to warn of foreseeable or latent dangers that might accompany the proper and intended use of the product.[19] With the courts continually expanding this concept, it is incumbent upon the manufacturer to insure that its products' labels are subject to a continuing review. A failure to do so might easily lead to a product liability judgment against the company because it has failed to warn properly.

From the court's standpoint, labels on which the manufacturers merely tell how to use the product but do not say anything about the danger of misuse do not adequately warn the public:

> Label on a weed killer warned that it contained sodium arsenite: "a strong poison—avoid contact with skin, eyes or clothing—when container is empty, immediately wash thoroughly and destroy." Manufacturer was negligent in failing to instruct as to disposal of rinse water and in failing to warn of delayed danger of poisons from disposal of residues, and was liable to plaintiff

> injured sunbathing on grass where rinse had been poured. With its experience and expertise, the defendant knew or should have known of the stable quality and long-lasting contamination propensities of the sodium arsenite contained in the triox solution upon the earth, and of the hazard or danger to humans coming in contact with such contaminated earth.[20]

In addition to labels, there are many other pieces of literature prepared by research and development in connection with a product, all of which have a direct bearing on the company's liability. These materials are subjected to the same scrutiny by the courts, and should contain proper directions on how to use the product safely as well as warnings of any hazards. Still another aspect of the problem is the action of research and development in complying with the many federal and state statutes on labeling, many of which outline the manufacturer's duty to warn, and in many instances contain minimum standards for labeling. If these standards are violated by the manufacturer, negligence per se or evidence of negligence is established, which could provide grounds for recovery in a product liability suit.

Statements made on labels have been held to impose warranties and liabilities on manufacturers when their products did not measure up to labeling claims. In one case, for example, labels on drums of insecticide containing traces of plant killer that could adversely affect production when sprayed on the plaintiff's cotton crop formed the basis of an express warranty. The labels, which bore a chemical analysis of the contents, were in effect representations that the ingredients listed were the only active ones contained in the spray. Failure to list the traces of the plant killer amounted to a breach of warranty.[21] In still another case, a manufacturer was held liable for the injuries of a man who had purchased certain tires in reliance upon a brochure extolling their safety features and road-clinging ability; one of the two-week-old tires had blown out suddenly and caused him to lose control of his car.[22]

Research and development departments in those companies whose products the courts refer to as "inherently dangerous commodities" have the duty of conveying to probable users of the products a fair and adequate warning of any dangerous potentialities. It is incumbent upon the labeling group of research and development to insure that all labels, brochures, and the like provide a fair and adequate notice of the possible consequences of use or misuse of the product. The courts have generally held that for a label to provide fair warning to the public it must be in a form that will (1) catch the attention of a reasonably prudent person, and (2) be understandable to the average user.

The following are a few examples of labels that the courts have found to be inadequate:

1. A label on "cement paint" warned that it was alkaline and might be injurious to sensitive skin after prolonged contact. It did not warn that a small quantity in the eyes would cause almost immediate blindness. The cautionary language on the label amounted to an assurance that the danger point was a safety point.
2. On the label of a cleaning fluid containing carbon tetrachloride and similar poisonous compounds, the only caution to users was to avoid breathing the fumes and to use in a well-ventilated place. An adequate label would have warned of the serious nature of the consequences of inhaling the fumes.
3. On a bottle of furniture polish, a warning that the

contents might "be harmful if swallowed, especially by children" was commingled with instructions for use and printed in 1/32-inch type.

The participation or supervision in the utilization of the product is another of the preventive activities of research and development in product liability. This can be a two-edged sword. It may on the one hand materially assist the customer by assuring the proper use of the company's product. On the other hand, if something does go wrong, the manufacturer is held to a higher standard of care because of the presence of its technical or marketing representatives. In many instances the very fact that the manufacturer maintains a research and development division subjects it to a greater degree of responsibility for care. The courts appear to have a tendency in such circumstances to hold the manufacturer liable because of its superior knowledge, particularly if a new product is involved.

Such a decision was given in an action by apple orchard owners against the manufacturer of an apple-scab spore-eradicant for damage to their apple orchard that had allegedly resulted from an application of the defendant's eradicant. Judgment for the plaintiff was set aside by the appellate court, but the Supreme Court of Virginia restored the judgment. It found, among other things, that

1. Adequate warning had not been given as to the consequences of an improper use of the product.
2. The conflict between the language on the label and that contained in a pamphlet constituted a violation of statutory requirements that manufacturers of economic poisons give directions for use and warnings as to any danger involved in using the product.[23]

Interestingly enough, a strong dissent pointed out that no injury would have occurred had the plaintiff observed the directions and caution statements on the label and pamphlet.

Manufacturers are required to exercise reasonable care in the design, development, construction, and assembly of products, in order to keep their products free from latent or hidden defects and avoid an unreasonable risk of harm to users. Design and development defects caused by inadequate or defective specifications or choice of materials have rendered manufacturers liable.

One of the leading cases that decided this point was a 1962 California decision,[24] a landmark case in the "strict liability" field. Here the plaintiff saw a home power shop demonstrated by a retailer and studied a brochure prepared by the manufacturer. His wife bought the machine for him for Christmas, and after he used it for a while, a piece of wood flew out of the lathe and struck him on the forehead. The plaintiff introduced expert testimony that his injuries were caused by defective design and construction of the equipment. From this testimony, the jury could reasonably conclude that the manufacturer had been negligent in constructing the equipment, and that the statements in the manufacturer's brochure were untrue. The court in this case held that a manufacturer is strictly liable in tort when he places an article on the market knowing that it is to be used without inspection for defects and it proves to have a defect that causes injury to a human being.

There is also a "defect" in the traditional sense when the product has been produced contrary to the intentions or representations of the manufacturer and contrary to the reasonable expectations of the consumer. In such instances, the product is truly "defective" within the rule of strict liability, and if the defect creates an unreasonable risk of harm, liability does follow. This rule has been applied in a number of cases that were decided on a theory of strict liability in tort—cases involving, for example, a mechanically defective braking system,[25] a defectively manufactured overhead guard on a forklift truck,[26] and a defective wheel on a wheelchair.[27]

Another effective method by which research and development contributes in the precomplaint field is the service that it provides in its technical library. This is a principal source of material in developing background data on complaints and litigation. In addition, the regular technical bulletins issued by research and development serve to educate the marketing field representatives in the various aspects of the company's products. This technical support, together with an aggressive research and development program and sound product development will materially lessen the exposure of the company to the dangers of losses in the product liability field. It is vital that the research operation be a never ending process that maintains pace with other aspects of the company's operation, so that products subjected to claims and litigations can be well researched and well defended.

In Chevron Chemical Company, Ortho Division, the products liability department has worked very closely with research and development in establishing safeguards to avoid the hazards of product liability complaints and lawsuits. Ortho, like most large manufacturers, is a so-called target company, and with increased legal activity in this field it anticipates that it will be named defendant in a certain number of lawsuits annually. As with other manufacturers, its share of the influx has increased gradually, reflecting the overall trends in the product litigation field. Whether this upward trend is inevitable cannot at this time be determined. What is certain is that most courts appear to be saying to manufacturers, "You who can absorb the loss should anticipate such losses and include them in your cost of producing the product—regardless of the legal liabilities." It is evident that the manufacturer or its insurance carrier must adopt a realistic claims philosophy in the face of these developments.

In the chemical field, and more particularly in the agrichemical field, research and development oversees a wide variety of activities in the period between initial development of a product and its successful commercial use in the field. In the event that litigation results from the sale of a product, each step in the procedure is subjected to the scrutiny of legal experts. Any shortcomings in the formulation, registration, labeling, manufacture, or sale of the product could well lead to liability on the part of the manufacturer.

Like other manufacturers, Chevron Chemical Company has initiated steps through its research and development department to minimize its exposure and reduce the company's appearances in court. One of the most important factors is the development of an awareness by all its personnel of the many facets of product liability. The objective here is to attain an attitude that permits the individual employee to consider the effect of the end product upon the public, even though he is involved in only one phase of the product's development. For example, the labeling department must be fully cognizant of all the hazards and dangers involved in each product so that the final label is complete and provides full protection to the ultimate user.

Another vital factor is the necessity for research and development to work closely with the advertising department in developing the advertising program and materials. It is a basic responsibility of research and development to insure that the TV, radio, and magazine advertising of Ortho's products accurately describe the function of the product. All copy is carefully gone over by the research and development staff before it is released by advertising. This is also true of other written materials, such as brochures and fliers, that are used as part of the advertising campaigns.

Efficient internal processing of product liability complaints is still another method of restricting litigation. It has been Ortho's experience that prompt response to inquiries frequently prevents the inquiry from becoming a complaint and the complaint from becoming a lawsuit. Results of analyses of product samples submitted in conjunction with a complaint are expedited from research and development laboratories through the claims department, back out to marketing, and then to the customer. If any deficiency or contamination is disclosed through the analyses of the product, corrective action is undertaken to avoid a recurrence.

Insurance companies play a vital role in the product liability field, and despite their efforts to control losses, the premiums continue to mount. The extent to which an insurance company is instrumental in aiding the individual company is directly related to the company's insurance program. Many larger companies are self-insured and must therefore generate their own safety programs. On the other hand, safety engineering departments of large insurance carriers have the advantage of wide experience in servicing a wide variety of companies and are in a position to put this know-how to use in helping the manufacturer to solve his problems.

3

Discovery and Disposition: Complaint Investigation and Termination

THE investigation of product liability complaints by research and development runs the gamut from brief, cursory, superficial comments on a simple complaint to extensive, detailed, time-consuming investigations of complex claims. The latter are more likely to occur when the reputation of one of the company's leading money-makers is at stake. Various steps are taken to head off a minor complaint in order to keep it from developing into a major piece of litigation, and the most important step is a prompt acknowledgment of the customer's problem.

Generally, most customers who initiate complaints are merely seeking answers. A response from a technical representative of the company carries considerable weight, and on occasion will serve to terminate the complaint before it develops into a legal action. Different industries require their research and development departments to take different steps in the development of their investigations. Basic to most plans is an analysis of the product, if the product is available, supplemented by laboratory or field tests as necessary.

Whenever a claim based on the company's product reaches the litigation stage, company counsel reviews thoroughly all steps taken in the development, production, and marketing of the product, and scrutinizes each phase to determine whether it will stand up under the cross-examination of a trial. The principal items in his examination are as follows:

1. Sampling procedures. The nature and type of the product; the extent to which it was sampled in the field and the laboratory; the nature and area of sampling; and the hazards and side effects, if any.
2. Labeling. The clarity and precision of cautions and warnings.
3. Production. The extent of quality control exercised; the sampling procedures during production; the nature of the facilities; and the retained batch samples.
4. Packaging. The strength and effectiveness of all parts of the product container.
5. Records. Production, research and development, and formulation.

Sampling Procedures

The success or failure of many a product liability investigation may well be contingent upon the validity of research and development's sampling procedures. In many cases, the original product sample may not be obtained by a representative of this group. However, when the sample does arrive at the research and development laboratory, its handling must be above suspicion and doubt, and clear and precise records must be maintained from the day it arrives to the final analysis. There must be no grounds for a claim that the sample does not truly represent the product under scrutiny.

It must be stressed that a proper sample is of vital importance in most cases. The danger in sampling is that it is such a routine procedure that carelessness creeps into the operation. The manufacturer must be able to convince the jury through analysis of the sample that the product is defect-free, and that it meets all specifications of the product. This cannot be underestimated in the mind of the jury. Defense must also be able, through research and development representation, to establish the nature of the handling and storing of the sample at various stages in its custody. A test or a chemical or physical analysis can be no better than the sample on which the analysis is performed.

In some cases the method used by technical people is to analyze a small sample, ideally a portion or part of the original product. However, if such a sample is not available, the results of an analysis of a retained batch sample obtained at the time of manufacture can be effective in court. This method is frequently resorted to in the agricultural, chemical, and related fields in which the product is completely consumed before the legal action. Great care should be exercised to establish that the research and development laboratory people know why the sample is being submitted. Merely arranging to have analyses run is not sufficient; the laboratory should be made aware of the nature of the claim. The best practice is to have a copy of the product liability complaint available for review.

Of course, certain practical limitations—such as cost, time, and interference with other demands—exert some influence on the amount of analytic work that can be performed in connection with the product liability claim. Any analysis that is done must be necessary for the successful defense of the action. Furthermore, although there is in most instances no ratio between the cost of the analysis and the cost of the product, there should be some relationship between the cost of the analysis and the company's exposure in the case. Quite obviously, several hundred dollars' worth of analytical work is not called for in a minor property damage claim.

Liability Claims and the Sales Force

Another important role played by research and development is that of technical counselor and adviser to the marketing sales force. Complaints or claims reach the manufacturer in many ways, but the most common is through the sales or marketing personnel. Many companies send out a technical adviser as part of a salesman's training program, and conduct follow-up seminars to insure that the members of the sales force have background and knowledge of all new products as they become available to the public. This continuing educational process by a technician from research and development is an important preventative to product liability claims. Although it is an established fact that one of a company's greatest liability exposures is its sales force, a well-trained sales staff should greatly reduce the number and size of product liability claims. If the men can see and understand the "red flag" of a potential claim in its early stages, and call upon the technicians for help, much can be done to mitigate the seriousness of the company's exposure.

In some industries, particularly in the petrochemical field, the company's products are utilized with other chemicals according to the recommendations of the sales force. Here again, research and development enters the picture. Erroneous recommendations by field sales representatives can lead the company into additional claims. In this area research and development serves two preventive functions: (1) the preparation of technical literature, labels, and pamphlets upon which the sales force must rely; and (2) day-to-day consultations. An experienced salesman recognizes when he is in over his head and should consult with research and development representatives before he makes a recommendation about which he is uncertain. Often, the technical adviser should go beyond a simple consultation by making a field examination to insure proper utilization of the product and to prevent the possibility of a product liability claim. Under such conditions, research and development is in a position to advise not only company personnel but the customer as well about the hazards involved. This procedure is especially effective when new products are being sold.

One procedure adopted by some companies is to have its technical staff conduct meetings for its customers similar to those conducted for the sales force. All the usual illustrative tools are relied upon to make clear to the consumer the use to which the product is to be put, stressing the hazards as well as the selling points. One caution here is to make certain that the lectures do not become too "technical," leaving the customers with misconceptions. Opening up such a channel of communication may be important if problems arise at a later date, and also establishes a relationship that the research and development representative can put to good purpose if he has to conduct a formal product liability investigation.

The Case of the Expensive Walnuts

Not all individuals who sue a company are poor, uneducated, defenseless people being taken advantage of by a large corporation—as most plaintiffs' attorneys would like to have the jury believe. In one case, the defendant company recognized from the start that it had a highly competent adversary who was not only both wealthy and educated but also quite experienced in testifying in court.

The plaintiff, a walnut grower and commercial applicator of many years' experience, was also the past president of the state association of walnut growers and maintained a walnut orchard of approximately 96 acres. The grower claimed to have worked out a spray program with the company's sales representative in 1962. Shortly after the application, he had reported to the sales representative that the spray program had not been effective and, in fact, that the walnut meats were shriveled and discolored. In the beginning, as is typical in many of these lawsuits, the grower was interested only in finding out what had happened, and was not pressing a claim against the company. But because he found untenable the company's position that the spray program had not caused the damage, litigation followed soon after.

The company, through its research and development department, undertook extensive investigation, testing, and trial preparation. As a result, the company concluded that the grower's current troubles resulted from many problems facing his orchard over the years, both prior and subsequent to the 1962 spray application. The company recognized that the field man had not made a sound recommendation. In fact, company research and development experts who testified during the trial admitted that the program was not a sound one. However, all agreed that the program had not in itself caused the damage to the orchard. This proved to be the most difficult part of the case. The decision was made to fight the grower's claim, since the company concluded that the product was not at fault.

A three-week jury trial resulted, during which both sides introduced numerous witnesses and much demonstrable evidence such as pictures, charts, and graphs. The company relied heavily on research and development experts, both independent and in-company, to prove that the orchard had suffered from many conditions that could have caused its decline, none of which was related to the spray program.

During the course of the trial, evidence was introduced that favored both the plaintiff and the defendant. The chemical company's people recognized that the labeling on the can, the ads, the failure to provide all the records, and the coincidence of the field man's recommendations with the sharp downturn in the orchard were not helpful to the case for the defense. They believed, however, that the company had established an overwhelming weight of evidence to the effect that the spray program had not been the cause of the plaintiff's loss. The jury obviously did not agree, and returned a sizable judgment in favor of the plaintiff. It is never really possible to determine accurately why a jury decides as it does but in a subsequent survey of the jurors in this case, the following comments were noted:

The spray program. The jury believed that other growers who used a different spray program did not have the same problem. This belief demonstrated the importance in product liability cases of finding other growers with identical problems who did not use the same chemicals under a similar spray program.

The evidence. The jury felt that there had been too much expert testimony. This will probably always be a problem in presenting a highly technical defense to a lay jury that is unable to understand much of what it hears. Under our present court system, there appears to be no answer to this problem.

The tests. Despite the evidence of extensive laboratory testing, the jury felt that the company had not made sufficient field tests. In most of these product liability cases, it is necessary for the company not only to prove that its product did not do the damage, but to go further and establish what did. The company thought that it had done so in this case, but apparently it had not done so to the satisfaction of the jury.

The Field Guide

The case cited above is illustrative of the many ways in which research and development can be of assistance to marketing and sales in this phase of the company's operations—but there are others. One of these is the preparation of a guide or outline to be followed by the sales representative in the event that he is called upon to take the initial technical steps of a claims investigation. At Ortho, research and development prepared a field problem guide (see Exhibits 1–5), designed to aid the sales representative and the grower or rancher in solving their field problems. It stresses many of the "basics" of a good product liability investigation: prompt reporting, ascertaining the cause, securing samples, taking pictures, and so on.

The guide contains charts and 55 basic questions that assist the field representative when he is faced with a product liability claim in the field. Research and development has provided him with the basic questions to be asked, and by referring to the wheel charts he can avoid asking

(*text continued on page 41*)

Exhibit 1. Field Guide Instructions

HOW TO HANDLE CUSTOMER COMPLAINTS

1. Investigate the problem promptly while early symptoms are still evident.
2. As a technically trained representative, it is important that you assist the grower or rancher in determining the cause of his problem. This is necessary so that emergency measures can be developed to minimize his problems and so that a recurrence can be prevented.
3. Do not destroy affected crops until a full study of the problem has been made. Crops frequently will "grow out" of their problem.
4. Be prepared to take color pictures, since a good photograph showing early symptoms may help in the solving of the problem later when all symptoms have been observed.
5. Carry empty jars and bags so that samples of products or plants involved can be obtained with a minimum amount of effort, for analysis by chemists or biologists.
6. Use the questions in this guide when interviewing persons concerning field problems. Be thorough and don't hesitate to ask additional questions that you may have in your mind. Some suggested questions in this guide may not apply to specific problems.
7. Be sure to obtain the names and addresses of all persons who have examined the problem. List any opinions that were given.

Exhibit 2. Field Guide Outline of Questions and Instructions

1. List all products and rates used per acre. (Include details on wetting agents, etc.) How much water or oil was used per acre? List any previous treatments made this season. Do these uses agree with label recommendations? Exceptions?

2. List the order in which materials were added to the spray tank. (Include wetting agents, etc.)

3. Record all batch numbers involved. Obtain samples of undiluted products, both company and competitive. (Also collect any residues that exist on nozzles or screens.)

4. What material was previously used in the applicator? How long ago? Was equipment thoroughly cleaned out between treatments?

5. What is the source of water used (well, ditch, lake, etc.)? Is it hard water? What kind of oil was used (diesel, fuel, etc.)?

6. What is the approximate temperature of the water or the oil that was used in this mixture?

7. Has material been exposed to freezing weather or to extreme heat?

8. How long was diluted spray held before application was made?

9. Check on availability of forage and product samples and be ready to ship materials if necessary.

10. List number of acres (or animals) involved in this problem.

11. Was the product stored near weed killers?

12. Describe the product. (Color, oil globules on top, settling out, undissolved particles, lumps, grittiness, excessive dustiness, etc.) Does the product have a typical odor?

13. Is there sign of container breakdown, sediment, or water contamination?

14. Describe the diluted spray mixture. (Is it greasy, milky, separated, or full of undissolved materials?) How long does the diluted spray remain uniform? Does it clog screens or nozzles?

15. Is the container rusted or dented? Is there evidence of cap lining deterioration? Has the material been transferred from the original container?

16. Is there indication of exposure of product to air, stain by water, or compaction problems during storage?

17. Does the product have normal density? (Do filled bags have normal amount of air space?)

Exhibit 2 (continued)

18. Is there variation among containers of this same product?

19. What is the type and condition of sprayer used? How much agitation occurred during and after filling? Are nozzles in good condition? What was the spray pressure used? Was coverage inadequate, adequate, or excessive?

20. Give name and condition of application equipment. Did good flowability occur? Was coverage uniform and adequate?

21. Describe temperature, wind, humidity, and rainfall before, during, and after treatment.

22. Describe conditions when exposure occurred. Was the worker in a dense orchard canopy? Did equipment break?

23. How were animals exposed to spray? Were animals in the field at time of treatment? Did they eat treated crops or were they hit by spray drift?

24. Give names of workers who mixed and applied materials. Give date and time of day when treatment was made.

25. What is the crop, variety name, and stage of crop growth involved?

26. Was certified seed used? What was percent germination on seed bag label? Was the seed treated? What is the source of this seed?

27. Were seeds exposed to freezing weather or to extreme heat or humidity prior to sowing?

28. What is the size and condition of the crop plants? (Use scale on back cover if necessary.)

29. List the soil type and describe the condition of the soil. (Organic matter, soil moisture, etc.)

30. Describe age, sex, and condition of animals.

31. List types and stages of insects or other pests involved. Describe control obtained.

32. Has insect migration into the treated fields been a factor here?

33. What diseases are involved? Describe the disease symptoms before and after treatment (nematode problems should be included here). Estimate disease control obtained.

34. Has the weather favored disease development during this treatment?

35. List the kind, size, and condition of weeds involved in this problem. Estimate the percent control obtained on each weed.

Exhibit 2 (concluded)

36. Describe soil conditions at treatment time, if preemergence treatment was used.

37. Describe height and condition of the crop plants. (Use scale on back cover if necessary.)

38. Describe the fertilizer and irrigation programs.

39. Are there indications of insect, disease, nematodes, weed, nutritional, or other problems?

40. Is there any indication of poor soil drainage or poor soil aeration?

41. What is the common recommendation for controlling this problem in your area? Has this product performed satisfactorily for this use on other farms? Has complainant had previous trouble? Is this grower a good farmer?

42. Are there any changes in cultural practice from last year?

43. Was a weed killer or soil fumigant used in this area during the past year?

44. Have weed killers been used in nearby fields? When?

45. What is the trend in general crop yields this year, compared with the past three years?

46. What is the crop yield history for the past three years on this farm?

47. What safety equipment was being used at the time of treatment? (Respirator, gloves, etc.)

48. Has this person been previously exposed to similar products? Any medical data?

49. How many days after treatment was the problem first noticed?

50. Describe the injury that occurred to seeds or seedlings. What plant parts are affected? Are there burning, yellowing, wilting, curling, or twisting symptoms? Did injury occur before or after seedling emergence?

51. What plant parts are injured? Is injury old or new growth? Does injury vary between upper and lower leaf surfaces? Is injury evident as burning, yellowing, wilting, or twisting?

52. Describe the symptoms. What aid was given victim? Where? Was a doctor called? Was a doctor's report prepared?

53. Refer customer to local poison control center for advice on antidotes. Report to your supervisor immediately.

54. Have you contacted a veterinarian? (Give name and address.) What were his comments?

55. Did a decrease in number or size of fruit occur? Will the grower's profits be decreased? Will future growth or yield of the crop be affected?

Exhibit 3. Wheel Chart for Questions 1-18

L = Liquid
W = Wettable
D = Dust or Granular

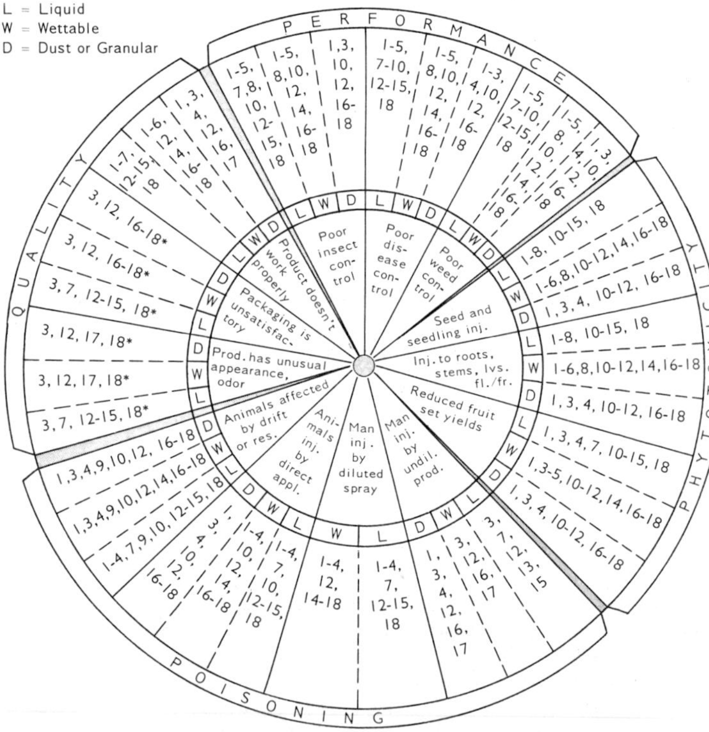

* Completes questions for this problem.

Exhibit 4. Wheel Chart for Questions 19-38

L = Liquid
W = Wettable
D = Dust or Granular

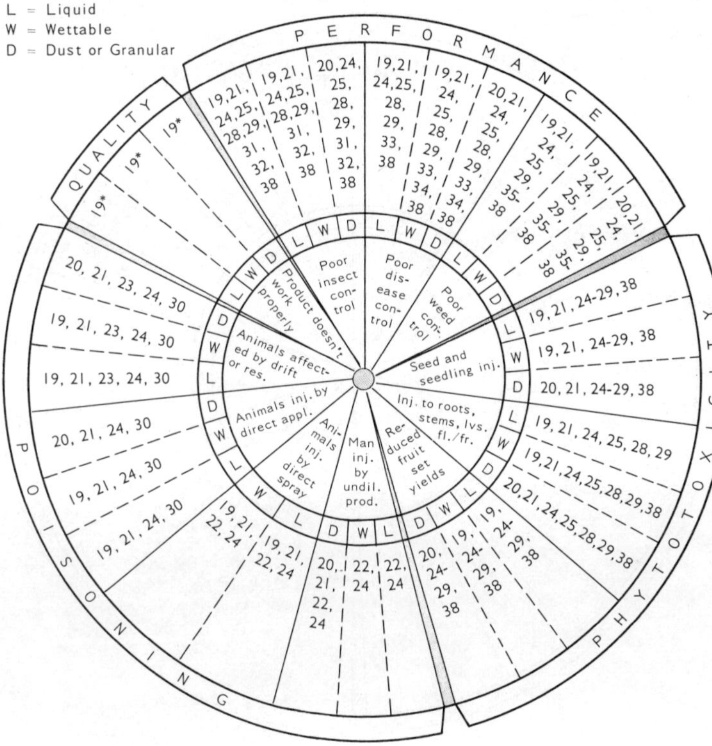

* Completes questions for this problem.

Exhibit 5. Wheel Chart for Questions 39-55

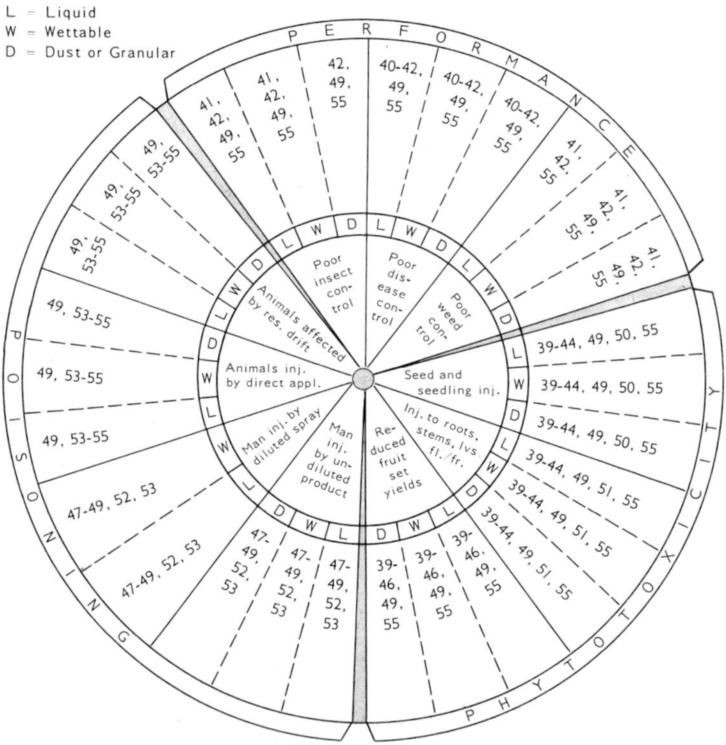

questions that are not pertinent to the problem at hand. While this sample guide is designed primarily for application in the agrichemical field, its basic tenets may well be applied in other industries.

In view of the large awards being made in product cases, it is incumbent upon the manufacturer's representative or his insurance carrier's adjuster to secure all the information early, before it disappears. For example, one recent suit involved a customer who purchased a gun and went off to Africa on safari to hunt wild animals. He was unsuccessful, because his new gun failed to fire after he had managed to sight his prey. He returned to this country and filed suit against the manufacturer of the gun, seeking to recover the costs of the safari and an amount for the loss of his personal prestige in failing to land the animal. The court, needless to say, agreed with him, holding that the label and advertisement for the gun were to be considered part of the sales contract and that they served as an express warranty to the purchaser of the gun's suitability for use in big-game hunting.

The Overall View

The product liability claims department has the responsibility of keeping research and development informed about developing trends in the products field. In an organization that has over 10,000 dealers and over 500 products in the field on a nationwide basis, it is essential to keep abreast of new legislation and litigation, and to convey such developments to key members of the research and development staff, particularly to those handling product registration and labeling.

It is also a well-known fact that both the plaintiff and

the manufacturer must become defense-oriented and freely cooperate in the exchange of data. In handling a product defect case, the attorney representing the plaintiff will attempt to trace the defect back to the manufacturer's corporate organization. One technique used is to take the deposition of a field representative and through him secure the names of all the key personnel in research and development. It is then a simple matter to obtain the deposition of all vital members of the staff in order to determine whether there is a communication breakdown within the department and at the same time reach the employee who is in charge of all safety aspects. In some companies, there may be no such person; in others, the plaintiff may be fortunate enough to encounter an incompetent. In either event, it will be much easier for him to establish defects in the product.

Manufacturers should review their corporate organizations to insure that they are receiving active management control of their product liability claims, either internally or through their insurance carrier. Ortho was recently sued in a southern state, along with 54 other companies, by a traveling salesman who had become exposed to a certain chemical over a ten-year period. All 55 companies either manufactured, formulated, or marketed the product that was the basis of the $250,000 litigation. The plaintiff's attorney had simply gone to the state Department of Agriculture, secured the name of every company registered to market or manufacture the product, and instituted suit against all 55 of them. What happened then was that a good many of the defendant companies or their insurance carriers made low compromise settlements—not because of the liability aspects, but simply to avoid legal costs. The plaintiff, in effect, recovered a sizable award without having to prove his case. Simply by bringing an action against a large number of defendants, he was able to convert his poor product liability case into a profit.

The position of the defendant manufacturers who chose to settle appears questionable. Certainly they were taking a very short-range view of a long-range problem. Pursuing a cause of saving litigation costs in the present will have the effect of encouraging multiple-defendant litigation in the future. Unless manufacturers achieve some form of cooperation in these "class" actions, all are going to wind up sadder, poorer, and wiser in the long run. The sad part of these settlements is that they never answer the important and relevant questions:

- Was the product defective?
- Was it properly labeled?
- Did it have adequate warnings?
- Was it properly tested by research and development?
- Were the 55 defendants at fault?

It is only when a sizable judgment is obtained against the manufacturer that management's indifference to this subject is shattered, and such judgments are on the way. A more equitable out-of-court result was obtained in a recent decision in the case of Julsruch v. Clairol Inc. Here the defendant did not settle the case, but through its attorney made a motion for summary judgment. The court granted the request, and found that the user, not the manufacturer, was at fault. The customer was found to be causally negligent as a matter of law, because she admittedly failed to make the requisite preliminary patch or skin test for hypersensitivity 24 hours in advance of each and every application of a hair tint. The court agreed with the manufacturer that the product had a warning on both the carton and the container, which said, "All users are to test their sensitivity to the product by making a preliminary patch or skin test." The judge further found the instructions and label that accompanied the product to be in compliance with the federal law. This decision was a clear victory for the defendant's research and development staff, which obviously did a thorough and detailed job in preparing the language to put on the cartons and containers.

Expert Testimony

Most members of the research and development department qualify as expert witnesses because of their formal educational backgrounds, although courts have permitted witnesses with little formal education to testify as experts if they have considerable practical experience. It is imperative that the witnesses be familiar with the aspect of the defense about which they are testifying, but their degree of specialization should not be such that it will limit the scope of their knowledge.

It is in the area of providing defense counsel with expert testimony that research and development performs one of its most valuable functions. Its personnel, because of their background and specialized training, are permitted to express their opinions in court—a right that few witnesses are allowed—and are deemed competent to testify, on the basis of the facts within their knowledge, as to whether a product is defective. For example, only a qualified expert could express the opinion that a design defect in the carburetor of an automobile was responsible for its improper operation.

The value of expert witnesses was made evident in the following Texas decision: An engineering company was conducting seismic exploration, creating the shock waves with dynamite charges set off by the company's employees. The charges used consisted of sticks of dynamite, a metal cylinder booster, and an electrical blasting cap, all three articles containing high explosives.

One day, the plaintiff, a driller's helper, was assisting a co-worker in drilling holes and preparing explosive charges. He secured five sticks of dynamite together and gave them to the driller, who punched a hole in the dynamite before inserting the booster and attaching the cap. The plaintiff walked 18 feet away to a truck to get a drink of water, and as he stood by the truck, the charge exploded, killing the driller and injuring the plaintiff severely.

As the court said, "The plaintiff's expert and lay witnesses advanced several hypotheses as to what probably happened." Actually, there was no proof as to the cause of the explosion, nor was there any proof that there had been a defect in the dynamite, the booster, or the cap. The plaintiff's expert advanced one theory of how the accident could have happened with defective dynamite, and another theory of how the accident could have happened with a defective cap. He stoutly maintained, however, that the booster had contained no fault. At the conclusion of all the evidence, the jury returned a verdict for the defendant companies.

On appeal, the United States Court of Appeals for the Fifth Circuit affirmed the decision with respect to the manufacturer of the metal cylinder booster, but reversed the decision concerning the manufacturers of the stick of dynamite and the blasting cap, and ordered a new trial. The ground of the reversal was that the trial court had erred in failing to charge the jury on the doctrine of "res ipsa loquitur." This doctrine simply means "the thing speaks for itself." In lay language, it means that when the defendant has exclusive control of the instrumentality, and the event would not normally have occurred without negligence, the burden of going forward with the evidence or expert testimony rests with the defendant. The important point to note in this case is that there was no evidence whatsoever of any specific defect in either the dynamite or the cap.

Consider the practical effect of this decision: Two component manufacturers go to a jury by order of the court of appeals, and the plaintiff has advanced theories, but no proof, as to the liability of each one. The jury under this holding would be entitled to bring back a verdict against either, neither, or both. Yet it is plain from the facts that if the dynamite was defective, the cap was not—and vice versa. On the record, the only means by which the jury could select either or both would be by speculation.[28]

In another case, it was alleged that a fire had originated in the motor of a refrigerator, and that this motor had been repaired negligently by one of the defendants. Although a refrigeration expert had reported to the plaintiff's testing laboratory that the fire had not been caused by the refrigerator, his report had been ignored. Subsequently, he was called as a witness by the defendant, and his testimony was found to be more convincing than that of the plaintiff's experts.[29]

Experience has shown that the decision in many lawsuits is directly related to the effectiveness of the parties' expert technical witnesses. Often, a lay jury is left with the unenviable task of deciding a product liability case in which conflicting scientific evidence is produced in court. It is apparent that the proponent with the ability to produce this scientific data in a manner that the jury can best grasp has a decided advantage.

The plaintiff often has the distinct advantages of possessing prior knowledge of the claim and exercising control over the product. In order for the defendant company to conduct an effective investigation of a product liability claim, it must assign its technical expert to the case as soon as the serious nature of the claim becomes apparent. Certainly, from a practical standpoint, not all product liability claims require the time and efforts of a technical member of the research and development group, but in most cases, if scientific experts are not promptly given the opportunity to study the product, valuable evidence is soon lost, particularly in chemical and drug claims.

It should be pointed out that, in addition to company experts, there are many other sources of expert assistance. One excellent source is the service of professional consultants from industry and the universities, although it has been found that many university people are reluctant to become involved in litigation. The use of this type of technical backup is strongly recommended, particularly in jury cases, because it lends support to the opinions expressed by the defendant's personnel.

Preparing a Case for Trial

Research and development plays an important role in the preparation of a case for trial—both as an adviser and as a source of information. Since courts of most states have begun widening their discovery procedures, the role of research and development has become critical, and many of its activities have become subject to the scrutiny of the plaintiff. Court decisions have been split over the extent to which the work of research and development is subject to discovery procedures. The courts appear to draw a distinction between the expert who is a company employee and an outside expert who is retained for trial.

Another function of research and development in the preparation and trial of a product liability lawsuit is the education of defense counsel. Because of the many advances in science and technology today, it is only rarely that a defense counsel will possess the scientific background to try a case successfully without expert guidance from the research and development group. This may mean time-consuming efforts on the part of research and development personnel to provide the company's counsel with the benefit of all their knowledge on a company's product. Only through the close cooperation between the legal and scientific members of the defense team can a company hope to achieve any measure of success.

It may be helpful to bring company counsel to the research and development facilities for a demonstration of all aspects of the company's handling of the product involved. Such a demonstration is invaluable in giving counsel an insight into the production and research problems, an insight which he can then convey to the jury through questioning and cross-examination of the witnesses. Some companies have also resorted to seminars attended by all its legal counsel and conducted by members of research and development.

Looking to the Future

At whatever stage the product liability complaint is disposed of, the research and development department should put into effect essential changes to avoid repetition of the complaint. These changes may be necessary within research and development itself—for example, in formulation, labeling, analysis, and testing. On the other hand, other departments such as manufacturing or marketing may have the primary responsibility. It is recognized that not every claim or lawsuit necessitates a change in methods and procedures. However, in the light of current trends in the product liability field, a company must remain flexible, and to ignore the danger signals subjects the company's profits to undue exposure to loss.

In summation, then, it should be made clear that new technical developments are coming at a more rapid pace than ever in most industries, and new products are being placed on the market more frequently than in the past. This situation, combined with government pressure, more liberal jury awards, and a greater awareness by the public, necessitates careful coordination between the research and development department and those within the company who have the responsibility of managing the company's product liability claims and litigation. An atmosphere of close cooperation must be maintained in order to insure aggressive and continual control in all stages of the complaints, and to allow for the successful defense of the claims. Both research and development and product claims must coordinate all activities that relate to the proposing, developing, and commercializing of new and improved products, in order to keep the channels of communication between the two clear and effective. Such a relationship may not stem the increasing flow of complaints, but it should in the long run permit the establishment of effective methods and procedures for controlling and minimizing losses in the product liability phase of the company's operations.

4

Two Agrichemical Case Studies

How Chevron Chemical Company, Ortho Division, has endeavored to implement the new relationship between product claims and research and development can best be illustrated by a case history. This test case will also illustrate the many pitfalls and travails that a manufacturer can face even if he produces a defect-free product.

Early in 1960, in a far western state, Ortho sold one of its products, Toxaphene DDT 4–2, to a local grower for the purpose of controlling certain insects in his cotton fields. This product had been used successfully in many states for many years without difficulty, and had been well researched and tested by research and development. However, the 1960 sale initiated endless investigative time for Ortho's research and development, manufacturing, marketing, and product liability personnel, as well as very high legal expenses involving two trials and an appeal to the Supreme Court of Arizona.

The basic contention of the customer in this product liability claim and in the lawsuit that followed was that he had purchased and applied Ortho's product, Toxaphene DDT 4–2, to his cotton crop by means of uncontaminated spray equipment. When the cotton suffered damage, he contended that Chevron Chemical Company was liable under the product liability claimant's usual theory that if damage is sustained after the use of the manufacturer's product, the manufacturer is liable. Such an assumption puts the onus on the manufacturer to establish through all the resources available to him that the damages resulted from other causal factors.

This Arizona crop damage case was primarily an investigation into the science of cause and effect. The customer's cotton crop was obviously damaged, and the investigation, two trials, and appeal all centered on a single factor—causation.

At the first trial in 1964, the superintendent of Ortho's pesticide-manufacturing department testified that in the summer of 1960 in Richmond, California, Toxaphene had been formulated in Ortho's plant No. 1, located about two miles from plant No. 2 in which 2,4–D and other weed killers were manufactured. No 2,4–D or other weed killers were formulated, stored, or permitted in Plant No. 1. On June 15, 1960, a batch of 3,010 gallons of Toxaphene was formulated. This batch was packaged June 16, 1960, in a hundred 30-gallon drums and two 5-gallon pails. A sample of this batch was taken, put in a bottle by research and development personnel, and given number 1215. The Toxaphene packaged that day was given code number R–21680.

A brief explanation of Ortho's code system is necessary. The "R" in the code number stands for Ortho's manufacturing plant at Richmond, California. The first number of the five-digit series (2) stands for the shift. The next three numbers in the series (168) refer to the day of the year, and the "0" at the end represents the year 1960. The code number R–21680 therefore shows that this particular batch of Toxaphene was packaged in Richmond during the day shift on June 16, 1960.

The manufacturing process for Toxaphene consisted in pumping it from the mixing tank to the packaging station and putting it into the drums by means of a straight pipe inserted directly into the bung hole. Only new drums unloaded at plant No. 1 were used in the packaging of Toxaphene.

On June 21, 1960, twenty-four 30-gallon drums of Toxaphene were shipped from Richmond to Phoenix, all the drums coded R–21680. About June 30, 1960, the customer purchased five 5-gallon cans and five 30-gallon drums of Toxaphene. About July 25, 1960, he returned to Ortho all the 5-gallon cans and two 30-gallon drums of Toxaphene and received credit for these items. Ortho admitted through its local sales representative that it had sold the Toxaphene to the customer for the purpose of controlling insects in his cotton, and that the product had been paid for.

The spraying of the cotton had been done by two of the cotton owner's employees. The deposition of the lead foreman was taken on January 10, 1963, more than a year before the first trial. In his deposition, the foreman (who had applied the chemical) repeatedly testified under oath that the first cotton field that he had sprayed with Toxaphene was the "A" field, one of the cotton fields that had suffered no damage. Before the cotton fields showed evidence of damage, the foreman had never heard of either Silvex or Kuron, and the owner had not cautioned him about their use. In his deposition, the foreman stated that he had used about one and one-half drums of Toxaphene on all the fields.

The other employee, the spray rig operator, gave his deposition on the same date. In his deposition he stated that he did not know what products besides Toxaphene were in the grower's storage shed; that he was unaware of any 2,4–D or Kuron in the shed; and that he did not remember the owner cautioning him about the danger of Kuron, Silvex, or 2,4–D to cotton. He was unable to remember how many batches of spray mix he could get from one 30-gallon drum.

Ortho had had nothing at all to do with the mixing or application of the Toxaphene, except to recommend the standard dosage as noted on the label. There was no complaint by the cotton owner about the recommendation. The spray rig, hand pump, measuring cans, water supply, and nurse tank trailer were all under the exclusive control of the claimant-owner and his agents. When not in use, the spray rig was kept in the owner's shed, the same shed in which the 2,4–D was kept and the Silvex and the Toxaphene drums were unloaded.

When the applicator finished spraying on the first night (July 2, 1960), he parked the spray rig in the field overnight by the nurse tank, also leaving the first opened 30-gallon drum in the field. When he resumed spraying the next day (July 3), he used the Toxaphene from this drum. In addition, according to the applicator, he left the spray rig, the nurse tank, and second opened drum of Toxaphene overnight in the field on July 3, and commenced spraying on July 4 with this equipment, covering about 15 acres. The claimant had three hand pumps on the ranch in 1960, all of which were of the same general nature and appearance.

About July 26, 1960, the cotton crop owner, the local

agricultural extension service man, and two marketing representatives of Ortho visited the storage sheds together. In and about the shed they found opened and unopened, empty, partially full, and full cans of 2,4–D and Silvex weed killers in close proximity to the Toxaphene drums. One of the hand pumps was lying over the Silvex weed killer cans. At this meeting, the owner expressed an opinion that it was possible that one of his applicators might have used a can of Silvex on the cotton by mistake.

The storage shed was the one in which the claimants unloaded and stored herbicides and insecticides. A standard precautionary measure to be taken by a farmer in handling 2,4–D and related weed killers such as Silvex is to store them separately from insecticides in order to avoid the possibility of contamination. The claimant did not take this precautionary measure.

The owner had told the applicator to apply one half-gallon of Toxaphene per acre with ten gallons of water, which was standard dosage. A full spray tank load contained about 7.5 gallons of Toxaphene and 143 gallons of water, which should have covered 15 acres. One 30-gallon drum of Toxaphene makes four spray tank loads, which cover 60 acres. In his deposition of April 4, 1962, the owner contended that he had suffered almost 107 acres of "burned" cotton. Using the recommended dosage on 107 acres would have consumed only 1.75 drums of Toxaphene. This fact agrees with the applicator's deposition testimony that he had opened only two drums. However, at the time of the trial, the claimant presented testimony that about 2.25 drums of Toxaphene had been used.

This discrepancy between the amount of Toxaphene used and the number of fields the cotton owner said had been sprayed indicated the spraying of additional acres with Toxaphene. Adding the 30 acres of cotton that the applicator said he had sprayed first without damages gave a total of 137 acres, which accounted for two full drums (on 120 acres) and the few acres he had sprayed from the third drum. In other words, the amount of Toxaphene used lent credence to the applicator's testimony that he had sprayed 30 acres of cotton with Toxaphene without any damage to the cotton. The evidence was confusing and conflicting as to where the new drums of Toxaphene had been opened and how much had been used.

The summons and complaint on this case were filed on November 22, 1961, and after usual discovery proceedings, the matter was scheduled for trial in Phoenix, Arizona, on March 16, 1964. At the trial, the cotton crop owner offered proof that his cotton had been damaged by two different chemical herbicides known as 2,4–D and Silvex, the latter known also by its brand name of Kuron.

Two qualified agricultural experts testified as to the damaged cotton that they had personally observed. These experts were an extension specialist in plant pathology and the research agronomist with the United States Department of Agriculture in Phoenix, Arizona. In addition, Ortho's plant pathologist and supervisor of biological research in research and development at Richmond, California, used the cotton owner's colored slides as evidence in describing the extent and cause of the damage. The testimony of these experts can be summarized as follows:

In the opinion of the extension specialist, the decreasing effect of Silvex was due to a diluting factor, so that the plants received less Silvex as the spraying continued across the fields. There were two different kinds of damage to the cotton, each caused by a different chemical, 2,4–D or Silvex. The experts gave their opinions that five gallons of Kuron dumped by mistake into the spraying solution would have caused the severe Silvex symptoms that they had observed on the cotton. It was also possible, they added, that a contaminated hand pump could have caused the moderate 2,4–D symptoms.

There was no doubt that the cotton was damaged. There was also no doubt that the damage had been caused by the two different chemicals, 2,4–D and Silvex. There was no evidence in the record to the contrary. The real issue in the case was the source of the contamination.

A standard scientific method of determining whether a particular product contains chemicals that will injure cotton is to apply samples of such a product to cotton and other delicate plants. Such biological tests offer more accurate proof of the product's effect on the plants than does a chemical analysis.

About July 26, 1960, the extension specialist and the local Ortho branch marketing manager took samples from the two Toxaphene drums at the storage shed. Both drums were milky, or emulsified, indicating the presence of water or some other foreign substance. On the same day, samples were taken from one of the several sealed Toxaphene drums of the same batch code number at Chevron Chemical Company's Phoenix warehouse.

The extension specialist gave his three samples to the USDA research agronomist with the request that he put them on test cotton plants according to the recommended dosage. The USDA expert performed the biological test by applying the three samples on three test cotton plants labeled according to the numbers on the samples. On examining the test plants, he observed that:

- There were no Silvex symptoms on any of the plants.
- The cotton painted with the Toxaphene from the drum in Ortho's warehouse was normal.

- The two cotton plants painted with the samples from the emulsified Toxaphene drums in the cotton owner's shed showed 2,4–D symptoms in different intensity (moderate from the almost empty drum and slight from the partially full drum).

From an examination of the projector slides that the extension specialist took of the test cotton plants, Ortho's plant pathologist reached the same conclusions.

Ortho's expert scientist performed a standard, scientific, biological test at Ortho's biolaboratory at Richmond, California, on the retained batch sample taken from the 3,010-gallon batch that had been packaged on June 16, 1960, in the drums labeled R–21680. This test consisted in spraying varying strengths of the retained batch samples on test cotton and other plants. At the same time, as a control factor, known amounts of 2,4–D were applied on similar plants. At the conclusion of these tests, there was no evidence of 2,4–D or Silvex in the retained batch sample.

As part of its investigation and trial preparation, Ortho brought its Phoenix counsel to Richmond for a two-day period to review all aspects of the case with research and development. At the completion of the review, it was concluded that this was a case of no liability, that Ortho had a good defense, and that the lawsuit should be permitted to go to trial. The two-week jury trial, begun on March 16, 1964, resulted in a unanimous verdict for the Chevron Chemical Company.

The plaintiffs, relying on the doctrine of res ipsa loquitur, did not attempt to present evidence of negligent manufacture or take any pictures of the manufacturing plant or processes. At the conclusion of the grower's case, the judge took Chevron's motion for a directed verdict on all three counts under advisement, and at the end of the trial he granted Chevron's motion on the plaintiff's third cause of action for negligent manufacture, holding the doctrine of res ipsa loquitur inapplicable under the facts. However, he denied Chevron's motion on the first and second causes of action on express and implied warranty.

On July 3, 1964, the cotton owner filed a notice of appeal in this matter, and in September 1968 the Supreme Court of Arizona awarded him a new trial, holding that the doctrine of res ipsa loquitur applied to the factual situation. The court found that:

> Although defendant [Chevron Chemical Company] no longer had exclusive control of the insecticide at the time of the spraying, the doctrine of res ipsa loquitur was nevertheless applicable where plaintiff showed that the insecticide came in sealed drums which were not unsealed until just before their contents were added to the spray solution, and that the herbicide contamination did not come from water or the plaintiff's spraying equipment.

This decision appears to have overlooked the fact that in a very narrow sense the damage to the cotton was caused by two different herbicides known as 2,4–D and Silvex, neither of which was in the exclusive control of defendant. In a broader view the instrumentality that damaged the cotton was the spray prepared by the cotton owner's people.

The case was retried for one week starting on June 9, 1969, and a unanimous verdict was again recovered by the Chevron Chemical Company, bringing to a close after nine years a claim based on a defect-free product. Lessons to be learned from this expensive product liability claim are numerous and worth repeating:

1. Specialists in research and development should be

consulted and brought into the early stages of any serious product liability claim.

2. All avenues of communication between research and development and the claims and legal departments should be kept open at all times—even for nine years.
3. Samples are essential and should be obtained and analyzed quickly.
4. Close coordination must be exercised between research and development personnel and defense counsel at pretrial and trial stages of the litigation.
5. There must be cooperation between scientists in research and development and those in federal and state agencies.
6. The defense of any claim requires research and development to work with and adjust to all the requirements and limitations of marketing and manufacturing.
7. A strong product liability claims philosophy must be developed and adhered to.

Still another case history illustrates the many problems besetting manufacturers. In this litigation, the plaintiffs sought \$100,000 for alleged "oil damage to walnuts" in two blocks (50 acres and 25 acres) of walnut trees interplanted with peaches. At issue in this litigation was the question of whether the Volck oil recommended by the Ortho sales representative for application to the peach trees in December 1962 caused the very apparent disease of the walnut trees, or whether these trees were damaged by frost, disease, or some other factors. Again, the crux of Ortho's defense was the technical assistance by representatives of research and development during the investigation and court trial.

During the 1962–1963 season, the Ortho sales representative made a standard recommendation of a chemical spray to the grower's peach trees. The manager of the orchard was advised not to spray the walnuts. The 50-acre section of the orchard had been planted with 1,240 walnut trees early in 1958. The walnut trees were planted on 40-foot squares, and were interplanted with peach trees planted in 20-foot squares, except for the substitution of a walnut tree for every other peach tree in every other row. A severe freeze in November 1958 resulted in the need to replant some 600 trees in January 1959, and there were additional replantings later on. The 25-acre block was planted solidly with peaches in the spring of 1958, and in 1961 it was interplanted with walnuts. Peach trees were not removed for this interplanting; the walnuts were simply put in the center of every other 20-foot square of peach trees.

At the time of the alleged damage in late 1962, the orchard had approximately 15 percent of the original planting remaining; the rest of the orchard consisted of replants. The research and development experts found upon investigation that the soil was tight and that the trees appeared to have been neglected. There was little evidence of sound efforts to prune, control pests, or irrigate.

The suit brought in 1964 charged Ortho with breach of warranty, strict liability, negligent manufacture, and negligent misrepresentation. The main contention of the grower was that the spray in question was not suitable for a peach orchard interplanted with walnut trees. The misrepresentation claim was based on the advice from the Ortho sales representative that the peach spray was safe for use in an orchard interplanted with walnuts. The grower stated that the damage had first been noticed in the spring of

1963, and that the Ortho sales representative had been notified. Upon examining the orchard, he had allegedly made the following remarks: "Well, looks like we burned your trees," and "It is definitely an oil burn." However, the Ortho sales representative denied having made these statements, and the jury in its final verdict accepted the veracity of the sales representative's denials.

In preparing this matter for trial, the chemical company performed extensive tests and studies, calling in independent experts to supplement the work of its own research and development experts. These studies revealed that the orchard exhibited signs of extremely poor cultural practices, low-grade soil, and several diseases, all of which had produced a tremendous mortality rate in the walnuts over a period of years. Extensive photographic work was done to highlight these conditions, and detailed charts and graphs were prepared. The company plant pathologist estimated that 50 percent of the trees had at least one infection, and that the damage was not the result of the spray, but rather of a combination of frost and disease superimposed upon inherently unhealthy trees. These findings were supported by the work of an independent plant pathologist from a local state college.

A two-week trial was held in early 1966, and after much deliberation, the jury awarded a defense verdict to the company. The plaintiff's attorney had submitted a $35,000 offer to settle the case shortly before the trial began. In the opinion of Ortho's defense counsel, three main factors contributed to the favorable decision:

1. Inability of the plaintiff to come up with any other instance of damage from a similar spray in the local area, where it was widely used.

2. Photographs exhibited to the jury during the trial, which depicted the generally poor condition of the plaintiff's orchard.
3. Creditability of the research and development expert witnesses.

The lesson from this case reaffirmed that old adage that "one picture is worth a thousand words." While the litigation proved to be expensive to defend, it again established the fact that, with immediate and sound factual investigation, and through the use of all research and development personnel and facilities, a company can overcome the many obstacles inherent in a product liability case.

Notes

[1] *The Wall Street Journal,* October 1, 1969.
[2] *Tennessee Law Review,* Spring 1957.
[3] Seeley v. White Motor Co., 63 A.C. 1.4 (1965).
[4] Santor v. A. & M. Karagheusian, Inc., 44 N.J. 52 (1965).
[5] Chapman Chemical Company v. Taylor, 215 Ark. 630 (1949).
[6] Magee v. Wyeth Laboratories, Inc., 214 C.A. 2d 340 (1963).
[7] Ross v. Philip Morris Co., 328 F. 2d 3 (1964).
[8] Garfield v. Atlantic Coast Line RR, 197 S.O. 2d 545, Flee. App. (1967).
[9] Sheward v. Virtue, 20 Cal. 2d 410, 126 P. 2d 345 (1942).
[10] Workstel v. Stein Bros., 156 N.Y.S. 2d 335 (1956).
[11] C. D. Herme Inc. v. R. C. Tway Co., 294 S.W. 2d 534, Ky. (1956).

[12] Gonzales v. Virginia Caroline Chemical Company, 239 Fed. Supp. 567 (1965).
[13] Hopkins v. E. I. du Pont de Nemours & Co., 199 F. 2d 930 (3d Cir. Pa., 1952).
[14] 346 U. S. 15, 73 S. Ct. 956, 97 L. Ed. 1427 (1953).
[15] Parker v. Ford Motor Co., 296 S.W. 2d 35, Mo. (1956).
[16] Elbers v. General Chemical Co., 310 Mich. 261, 17 N.W. 2d 176 (1945).
[17] M. Miller Co. v. Central Costa Sanitary Dist., 198 Cal. App. 2d (1962).
[18] Butler v. L. Sonneform Sons, Inc., 296 F. 2d 623, N.Y. (1961).
[19] Reynolds v. Natural Gas Equipment, 184 Cal. App. 2d 724 (1960).
[20] Boyl v. California Chemical Company, 221 F. Supp. 669 (1963).
[21] Burr v. Sherwin Williams Co., 42 Cal. 2d 682 (1954).
[22] Hansen v. Firestone Tire & Rubber Co., 276 F. 2d 254 (1960).
[23] McClanahan v. California Spray-Chemical Corp., 75 S.E. 2d 712 (1953).
[24] Greenman v. Yuba Power Products, Inc., 377 P. 2d 897 (1962).
[25] Vandermark v. Ford Motor Company, 391 P. 2d 168 (1964).
[26] Delaney v. Towmotor Corp., 339 Fed. 2d 4 (1964).
[27] Putnam v. Erie City Manufacturing Co., 338 Fed. 2d 911 (1964).
[28] Dement v. Olin Mathieson Chemical Corp., 282 Fed. 2d 76, C.A. 5 (1960).
[29] Pearl Insurance Co. v. Reily, 127 S.O. 2d 266 (1961).

About the Author

FRANK C. JOSE, JR. is manager, product liability claims, with the Chevron Chemical Company of the Standard Oil Company of California in San Francisco. He attended Rutgers University in New Jersey and in 1951 received a Doctor of Law degree from Rutgers Law School. Before joining his present firm, Dr. Jose was associated with Liberty Mutual Insurance Company for ten years. He is the author of several articles dealing with product liability claims.